Community College Assessment

Edited by Trudy W. Banta

Assessment
UPdate
COLLECTIONS

Published by Jossey-Bass
A Wiley Imprint
989 Market Street, San Francisco, CA 94103-1741   www.josseybass.com

Jossey-Bass books and products are available through most bookstores. To contact Jossey-Bass directly call our Customer Care Department within the U.S. at 800-956-7739, outside the U.S. at 317-572-3986, or fax 317-572-4002.

Jossey-Bass also publishes its books in a variety of electronic formats. Some content that appears in print may not be available in electronic books.

Library of Congress Cataloging-in-Publication Data available upon request

Printed in the United States of America
FIRST EDITION
PB Printing   10 9 8 7 6 5 4 3 2 1

Contents

Introduction: Assessment in Community Colleges

Trudy W. Banta

As many regular readers of *Assessment Update* know, one of the leading experts on community college assessment is Jeffrey A. Seybert, a frequent contributor to *Assessment Update* and director of research, evaluation, and instructional development at Johnson County (KS) Community College. For years Jeff and I have had a running debate about whether it is harder to make headway with outcomes assessment at research universities or at community colleges.

I will say, "At research universities we have faculty immersed in their research who are rewarded more for their scholarly achievements than for their teaching, and certainly more than for their impact on student learning! We have hundreds of degree programs, from two-year professional programs to Ph.D.s and even post-doctoral credentials. Our students—in some cases, as many as 50,000 of them on a single campus—are surely as diverse as yours, ranging from talented teenagers who may still be high school students to retired grandparents returning for enrichment experiences. Often 50 percent or more of our baccalaureate graduates did not begin as freshmen with us but instead transferred to our institutions after spending one to three years on one or more other campuses. In addition to a rich variety of cultural backgrounds among our domestic students, we enroll substantial numbers of international students from countries around the globe. Our primary missions of teaching, research, and service, or engagement, take us in many different directions."

Then Jeff will respond, "Yes, but community colleges must juggle all these missions: providing first- and second-year courses for people who just want to see if college is a good choice for them, courses and programs that meet articulation standards and permit students to transfer to four-year institutions, vocational and technical education, remedial and developmental coursework, noncredit continuing education, contract training for business and industry, courses for special populations, and all sorts of responsive community service. Our faculty are focused on teaching—and how! Whereas faculty at research universities typically teach two courses per semester, instructors at community colleges teach four to six courses at a time. This leaves little time or energy for assessment!"

Jeff goes on, "I'll grant you that research universities have diverse student populations. But it's the huge range of academic preparation and educational objectives community colleges confront that poses our biggest obstacle in this connection. In a single classroom we may have a new high school graduate who just squeaked by with Cs and Ds and doesn't know whether he wants to be in college or not and a Ph.D. chemist who wants to update her skills. The new graduate may drop out before the course is over and not return for years, if ever. The chemist may feel she has fulfilled her goal after three courses and leave us for good. Have we failed either of these students? Traditional assessment measures of retention and persistence to graduation may seem reasonable when applied to academically prepared students who are committed to the goal of achieving a degree when they enroll, but I would argue that they are not the best measures of mission accomplishment for community colleges."

Jeff and I eventually agree that outcomes assessment is difficult in any setting! But I must admit that my conversations with Jeff and other community college assessment practitioners have given me a special appreciation for the assessment accomplishments in this arena. Knowing how little time community college faculty have to write for publication, I have been doubly grateful to receive manuscripts from them for *Assessment Update*. And knowing the vital role that community colleges play within higher education, I have always tried to have at least one article representing this sector in every issue of *Assessment Update*.

During the first seven years of *Assessment Update*'s history we had at least one, and often two or three, community college pieces in each issue. By 1995 I was convinced by the stories coming in from Miami-Dade, Mt. Hood, Lane, and Johnson County Community Colleges and Midlands

Technical College that community colleges were in the vanguard of colleges and universities doing serious work in assessing institutional effectiveness. In my *Editor's Notes* in the September-October 1995 issue (7:5, p. 3) I wrote, "Community colleges are prominent among the leaders in higher education in establishing indicators of their effectiveness, gathering benchmark data, and using findings to improve the satisfaction of students and other community constituents."

But by the end of the decade I was finding it harder to include a community college article in every issue because the manuscript flow had dwindled. And in 1999 Peterson and others published the results of a national survey that led them to conclude: "Most associate of arts institutions are not using student assessment data to make academic decisions" (p. 56).

What changed over the ten years between 1989 and 1999?

In the Peterson et al. study, questionnaires were mailed to the chief academic administrators at all (2,524) non-proprietary postsecondary institutions recognized by the U.S. Office of Education that offered undergraduate programs at the associate or baccalaureate degree level in 1998. Completed surveys were received from 1,393 (55 percent) of the institutions, including 548 (54 percent) associate of arts institutions. Peterson et al. state in their summary,

> . . . in comparing (them) to all institutions . . . associate of arts institutions are less likely to collect cognitive and affective data, less likely to use student-centered methods in collecting data, and less likely to conduct studies linking student performance to students' interactions with their institutions. Perhaps because associate of arts students are more likely to be attending part-time and to be commuting, it is more difficult to engage them in assessment activities. (p. 27)

I believe, and I think Jeff Seybert would agree, that just as community colleges have a head start on traditional four-year institutions in addressing stakeholders' demands for responsive programs and services, they also have led the way in demonstrating their accountability through the assessment of institutional effectiveness. They have set institution-wide goals and objectives for general education and transfer programs, vocational and technical education, remedial and developmental coursework, non-credit continuing education and contract training for business and industry. They have linked these plans with their budgets and developed relevant measures of progress and success. Then they have established systems for following student progress and transfer as well as performance and satisfaction of graduates.

But in the years from 1995 until now the focus in assessment in two-year as well as four-year institutions has moved from institutional effectiveness to student learning. Every institution is struggling with this because good measures of student learning are scarce. But focusing on student learning is particularly difficult in community colleges because students enter with such diverse educational goals and are so likely to stop out, transfer, or drop out. Not only is it "more difficult to engage them in assessment activities," as Peterson et al., hypothesize, it is also more difficult to engage them in their education. And as assessment at community colleges has become harder to do, fewer faculty are writing about it, and *Assessment Update* is receiving fewer manuscripts.

At this watershed in the history of community college assessment—when more two-year faculty and administrators than ever are searching for assessment methods of demonstrated value—it seems particularly important to collect between two covers some of the strongest illustrations of good practice that have appeared in the pages of *Assessment Update* over the years since its founding in 1989. Herein we provide examples of methods useful in assessing learning as well as institutional effectiveness in community colleges.

Following an overview by Jeff Seybert himself, we focus on the development of methods to assess the generic student outcomes that permit students to transfer to four-year institutions, since these are at the heart of the community college mission. Within this section you will recognize the age-old debate between those who advocate the use of standardized measures of student learning and those who prefer faculty-developed measures. In the last part of this section we have presented some examples of the compromise: that is, using a combination of the two.

Assessment of additional aspects of the community college mission is addressed in selections on transfer, vocational-technical programs, and specific skills.

Reasoning from the particular to the more general, we close with a section on assessing institutional effectiveness using instruments and benchmarking strategies that are national in scope. Fittingly, we turn again in this section to our resident authority, Jeff Seybert.

Reference

Peterson, M. W., Augustine, C. H., Einarson, M. K., and Vaughan, D. S. *Designing Student Assessment to Strengthen Institutional Performance in Associate of Arts Institutions*. Stanford, CA: National Center for Postsecondary Improvement, Stanford University, 1999.

Overview

How to Initiate an Assessment Program

Jeffrey A. Seybert

For those who are interested in learning more about how to get an assessment program started at a community college, here is some step-by-step advice from an authority in the field. From Assessment Update 5:2.

As I travel around the country talking to faculty and administrators at two-year colleges about assessment of institutional effectiveness and student learning outcomes, the single question that I am asked most often is "How do we start—what should we do to begin to implement an assessment process?" Thus, I present here a brief list of steps that I believe an institution may want to take to initiate an assessment program.

1. *Create an institutional effectiveness assessment task force.* This task force should be broadly representative of college faculty and administrators and should include (but not be limited to) a senior administrator (president, vice president, or dean of instruction) firmly committed to assessment, institutional research personnel, faculty, and student affairs staff. Committed faculty and upper-level administrative involvement are absolutely critical; I am firmly convinced that assessment cannot be successful without them. In addition, I think that this should be a perma-

nent task force whose job is to guide, evaluate, and modify the assessment effort as it evolves.

2. *Examine the college mission statement.* Assessment is essentially an examination of the degree to which the institution is in fact adhering in practice to the principles of its mission statement. Since the college mission statement is the standard against which institutional effectiveness will be measured, it is critical that the mission statement be up to date and fully reflect what the college is supposed to be doing. This examination may dictate a revision of the mission statement, depending on its currency.

3. *Design an institutional plan or model to guide the assessment program.* This plan may (or may not) be based on one of the four formal models that have been proposed as conceptual frameworks for assessment (see the Community College Strategies column in *Assessment Update,* 1992, 4 (4), 13). In any case, it is helpful to have a plan or model to guide the assessment effort so as to ensure that it addresses all major facets of the institution's activities and places assessment in some overall context.

4. *Determine and prioritize the specific assessments to be undertaken.* The priorities will depend on the immediacy of external mandates, internal needs for assessment data, and the like.

5. *Inventory existing data collection efforts.* Even in institutional research or assessment office, numerous data collection efforts are under way. Many of these can be incorporated into the assessment process.

6. *Determine what additional data collection procedures need to be implemented to inform the assessment priorities identified in step 4.* This step may require the implementation of additional data collection efforts. Implementation of an overall assessment effort will not generally occur without some new costs.

7. *Start at the top of the priority list.* Start small, with selected pilot projects in areas where faculty and staff are excited and ready to go.

8. *Be flexible, adaptive, and prepared to change.* There will always be problems; mandates, circumstances, personnel, and priorities can always change. Assessment must be viewed as dynamic and evolutionary and not as a static process that is set in concrete once it is fully implemented.

9. *Be prepared and willing to publicly share results of assessments.* Experience shows us that the results of these assessment procedures are almost always positive. They thus provide marvelous public relations opportunities and also help reinforce the commitment of faculty and staff who cooperated and participated in the assessment process.

10. *Keep in mind that the primary emphasis in assessment is on the improvement of teaching, learning, and services to students.* If assessment results are not used to make program and curriculum improvements, the entire effort is wasted.

As noted above, this is a *suggested* list of implementation steps. Individual institutions may want to follow this sequence, add steps, change the order in which the steps take place, or delete a step that is not applicable.

Finally, I want to emphasize that there is no one perfect model or sequence of actions that fits all two-year colleges. Each institution should design a model and course of action to address its specific needs and circumstances.

Jeffrey A. Seybert is director of research, evalutation, and instructional development at Johnson County Community College in Overland Park, Kansas, and serves as project director for both the Kansas Study and the National Community College Benchmarking Project.

Assessing Student Achievement of Generic Knowledge Skills

Report on a Pilot Study to Evaluate the Validity of Standardized Tests as Measures of Student Learning

Joint Task Force of the Interinstitutional Committee of Academic Officers and State Board for Community College Education

Can standardized tests be useful in assessing sophomores' skills? A pilot study in Washington State examined the use of three tests and came to the conclusion that they were in fact not useful. From Assessment Update 1:3.

The Washington State institutions of higher education have a long-standing commitment to assessing student learning and discerning the value of a college education. They agree that assessment helps enhance the quality of programs. Faculty and administrators across the state are currently involved in discussions and studies to determine the best methods for obtaining appropriate and useful information from assessment activities.

Some states use standardized tests to measure students' academic performance. The state Higher Education Coordinating (HEC) Board recommended in its master plans (Dec 1987) that two-year and four-year institutions conduct a pilot study to evaluate the appropriateness of using standardized tests as one means for measuring the communication, computation, and critical-thinking skills of sophomores. The purposes of such a testing program would be for institutions to strengthen their curricula, improve teaching and learning, and provide accountability data to the public.

To design and implement the study requested by the master plan, two task forces were established. One represented the public baccalaureate institutions, and the other represented the community colleges. Both task forces included faculty and academic administrators from each participating institution as well as two HEC Board members. The two task forces worked in parallel and ultimately conducted a joint study.

Only three tests met the criteria for the HEC Board's recommendation for the study: the Academic Profile, the College Outcome Measures Program (COMP), and the Collegiate Assessment of Academic Proficiency (CAAP). Over 1,300 sophomores from public four-year institutions and from eight two-year colleges were tested, and each student took two of the three tests. More than 10 faculty members from the same institutions took shortened versions of the tests and critiqued them for appropriateness of content and usefulness.

The results of the pilot study strongly suggest that the three tests do not provide an appropriate or useful assessment of the communication, computation, and critical-thinking skills of Washington college sophomores. None of the tests measured the separate academic skills (communication, computation, and critical thinking); rather, these tests primarily measured verbal and quantitative aptitude. Moreover, the tests added little reliable new information about students' academic performance. Results essentially reiterated what is already known from admissions test data and grades. Further, test scores were not sensitive to specific aspects of the college experience, such as estimated time spent studying and credits earned. Finally, none of the tests was judged by faculty as providing an adequate match with curricular content or as being an appropriate or useful measure of communication, computation, and critical thinking. Norms for making comparisons with peer institutions are currently unavailable. Furthermore, student performance is affected by differences in how institutions administer tests, in the timing of tests, in the selection of students, and in student motivation. Thus, comparisons with future norms which are based on tests given under differing conditions will be misleading.

Both two-year and four-year faculty participants in the study recognized the importance and value of having public as well as institutional access to appropriate measures of student performance. They reaffirmed the value of assessment activities for strengthening the curriculum, improving teaching and learning, and enhancing overall instructional quality. They also shared the view that the development of meaningful assessment measures is both difficult and time consuming, that measures should be institutional specific, and that national standardized, multiple-choice tests have serious limitations for the assessment of teaching and learning.

Assessing General Education Using a Standardized Test: Challenges and Successful Solutions

Jan A. Geesaman, Peter T. Klassen, Russell Watson

How can community colleges come up with reliable assessments of student learning when their student population is in constant flux? The authors, faculty and administrators at the College of DuPage, devised a way to use the six American College Test Collegiate Assessment of Academic Proficiency area tests to assess what students learned during their years at that institution. This approach can be used at two-year as well as four-year institutions. From As-sessment Update 12:6.

College of DuPage (34,000 students) in Glen Ellyn, Illinois, has developed a general education assessment design that can be used easily at two-year or four-year institutions of any size. This general education assessment model grew from the college's initial classroom assessment initiative, and now its second full year of implementation is complete. This article will review the assessment design, use of results to close the feedback loop, ways faculty cooperation was encouraged, and means of motivating students to give their best efforts during the assessment activities.

Assessment Design

A decade ago, two-year colleges were known for their "enrollment churn" and the attendant problems of attempting to use a pretest/posttest model for assessment of student learning. Now that same enrollment churn occurs at many four-year institutions. Because of this type of enrollment pattern at College of DuPage (COD), true pretesting and posttesting was unrealistic, and therefore a pseudo–pretest/posttest model was designed. This strategy involves administering the six American College Test/Collegiate Assessment of Academic Proficiency (ACT/CAAP) area tests to sections of introductory courses during the fall quarter, and to sections of advanced courses with primarily graduating or transferring students in the spring quarter. A stratified proportionate random sample of class sections is obtained and matched for distribution on day/night and on/off campus variables. In each class section used in the assessment process, each of the six CAAP area tests is administered to separate groups of students. That is, in a given section of thirty students: five students each take the Math, Science Reasoning, Writing Skills, Reading, Critical Thinking, and Essay Writing area tests. This method provides for the most representative assessment of general education skills in the student population.

A series of additional statistical controls helps maintain a robust examination of those students taking their college sequence at our institution. One control for the "freshman drop-out effect" involves removing scores from freshman students not registered at the college during the following spring quarter. Another control involves removing scores from those students who were tested during spring quarter but who had taken college credit at other institutions. With these and other controls for the "perpetual student," we were able to obtain a pool of entering freshmen who had completed either one or two years of classes at the college, and a pool of completing sophomores who had taken classes only at COD. In addition, there was a middle pool of midyear freshmen and sophomores who were approximately halfway through their COD experience. A more detailed discussion of the controls, results, and methodology is available at the COD assessment Web site at <www.cod.edu/outcomes/CAAP1999.htm>.

Use of Results

Typically, whenever assessment results are posted at an institution, an often-heard comment from many faculty is "What are we supposed to do with this?" For this initiative, we wanted to ensure that communication was a two-way process. Therefore, with each report of assessment results, a tear-off response sheet is included that may either be submitted or filed electronically through the college intranet. These response sheets ask multiple-choice, short-answer, and open-ended questions about what faculty members think should be done with the results of the assessment data and what they are going to do individually. Finally, written faculty responses are published (anonymously) in a follow-up document. This process allows not only maximum input but also maximum distribution of responses. While initial response rates were low, we have experienced a gradual increase in participation by faculty. Also, after initial responses were published, faculty dialogue about our efforts and results increased. Questions asked and faculty responses may be found on the Web site noted previously.

In fall 1999, results of the first phase of our ACT/CAAP assessment battery revealed that College of DuPage students scored, on average, lower than ACT two-year college norms in college-level reading skills. As a result, faculty in each division incorporated a reading-related goal in their area objectives. In fall 2000, the latest ACT/CAAP reading scores show a slight (though not statistically significant) increase in reading skills among sophomore students. This information will be shared at our fall faculty meeting with the message that while there was some increase in reading scores, continued emphasis needs to be placed on improving college-level reading skills across our general education curriculum.

Faculty Cooperation

Faculty opposition to giving up in-class time for any noninstructional purpose is universal, and assessment is no exception. However, a request to donate 50 minutes of class time for the purpose of achieving a greater understanding of students' learning in areas of general education skills usually elicits a higher level of faculty cooperation. College of DuPage has about 300 full-time and 1,200 part-time faculty. The selection of classes described earlier involves 30–35 sections each in the fall and spring. Since a list of randomly selected class sections is used, only 30 faculty from a pool of nearly 1,500 are solicited for each round of testing. Each faculty member thus has only about a 2 percent chance of being selected during each testing round. Given these circumstances and the fact that this assessment process is a faculty-driven initiative, our experience has been one of substantial cooperation. In fact, out of four rounds of ACT/CAAP testing to date involving about 2,400 students and about 120 faculty, only one faculty member has refused to participate.

Student Motivation

Another major challenge in using standardized testing as an assessment technique involves motivating students to give their best effort. Unsuccessful incentive systems have included providing discount coupons at the college bookstore, coupons for free pizza, tuition discount coupons, free meals, T-shirts, certificates of participation, and other inducements. The following method used at College of DuPage seems to have yielded appropriate and sincere participation by students. After the class sections are randomly selected, the instructor reads a letter to the class indicating that sometime during the next two weeks that class section has been asked to participate in the CAAP testing. In addition, the students are given a trifold brochure describing the CAAP tests, why they are important to the college, and why they should be important to students as individuals. This brochure asks the students to do their best on the test and tells them that they will receive their own results, which will give them a sense of their general education skills in a way that does not affect their classroom grades or grade point average. In addition, the students are informed that if their score exceeds the national mean, ACT will issue a certificate attesting to their performance. Finally, instructors of each class section selected to participate are asked to remain in the room during the testing period. It seems that the presence of their instructor is an additional incentive for students to perform well on the test. There are always students who fail to take assessment testing seriously; however, careful monitoring of completed CAAP answer sheets has revealed that those students account for only about 1 percent of participants at College of DuPage.

Conclusion

While few testing systems are ideal for all cases, the assessment committee has been very pleased with the design, faculty and student participation, and the usability (and use of results) of the assessment model at College of DuPage. Although our experience is still somewhat limited, this is a general education assessment model that appears to have overcome several of the major challenges associated with the use of standardized testing for assessment of general education outcomes and that could be adapted to any two- or four-year institution.

Jan A. Geesaman is associate dean of communications and a member of the assessment committee at College of DuPage. Peter T. Klassen is professor emeritus of sociology and interdisciplinary studies at College of DuPage and an assessment consultant in private practice. Russell Watson is professor of psychology and faculty chair of the assessment committee at College of DuPage.

The Community College Student Experiences Questionnaire

Gary R. Pike

Are there reliable measures available to assess the quality and quantity of student involvement that occurs at a community college? The author describes one measure—the Community College Student Experiences Questionnaire. He summarizes the results of studies that establish its validity and reveal the many ways it has been useful to faculty and administrators at community colleges. From Assessment Update 8:1.

My own bias is that any comprehensive assessment program should focus on what students do (that is, educational processes) as well as on what students learn (that is, educational outcomes). A similar philosophy is reflected in the National Center for Higher Education Management Systems report on using indicators of good practice in undergraduate assessment (see Ewell, Lovell, Dressler, and Jones, 1994). It also is reflected in the research of Pascarella, Terenzini, and their colleagues in connection with the National Study of Student Learning and in many of the surveys I have reviewed for *Assessment Update*. As Pascarella and Terenzini (1991, p. 610) noted in *How College Affects Students*, "One of the most inescapable and unequivocal conclusions we can make is that the impact of college is largely determined by the individual's quality of effort and level of involvement in both academic and nonacademic activities."

In an earlier issue of *Assessment Update* (Vol. 2, No. 1), I reviewed the College Student Experiences Questionnaire (CSEQ), developed by C. Robert Pace. In that column, I noted that the CSEQ has been used by a variety of four-year colleges and universities and that the quality-of-effort scales in the CSEQ provide important information about what students do in college.

While the CSEQ is a useful assessment tool for four-year institutions, it is not appropriate for two-year institutions. Many of the experiences in the CSEQ quality-of-effort scales (for example, Student Unions and Residence Halls) are not appropriate for two-year institutions. At the same time, experiences that are appropriate for students at two-year institutions (for example, experiences related to the development of vocational skills) are not included in the CSEQ.

Recognizing the limitations of the CSEQ for two-year institutions, Pace, Friedlander, and Lehman developed and published the Community College Student Experiences Questionnaire (CCSEQ) in 1990. Since its publication, the CCSEQ has been administered to more than 18,000 students at fifty-six community colleges nationwide. From 1990 to 1994, the CCSEQ was disseminated by Pace at the University of California-Los Angeles. Since 1994, the base of operations for the CCSEQ has been moved to the Center for the Study of Higher Education at the University of Memphis under the directorship of Patricia H. Murrell.

Friedlander, Murrell, and MacDougall (1993) surveyed representatives from twenty-six community colleges that have administered the CCSEQ. Uses of the CCSEQ have ranged from local institutional assessment and evaluation to statewide reporting and basic research on community college students. Examples of the ways in which CCSEQ data have been used in assessment programs range from making changes in specific courses to establishing new programs institutionwide. Specifically, English Department faculty at one institution found that a large number of students were not utilizing library resources effectively. The faculty subsequently modified several courses to include a component on using the library. Likewise, another school found that student involvement was extremely poor. The institution subsequently developed a component in its new student orientation program that focused on student involvement.

By far, the most significant change in the CCSEQ that distinguishes it from the CSEQ is the reduction in the number of quality-of-effort scales, from 14 in the CSEQ to 7 in the CCSEQ. The quality-of-effort scales in the CCSEQ are Course Learning; Library Usage; Interaction with Faculty; Student Acquaintances; Art, Music, and Theater; Science Activities; and Vocational Skills.

Like the 14 scales in the CSEQ, the quality-of-effort measures in the CCSEQ consist of Guttman-like items designed to measure both the breadth and depth of student involvement. For example, the quality-of-effort scale on course learning includes questions related to the number of times the respondent participated in class discussions, summarized major points and information from readings or notes, studied course materials with other students, compared different points of view presented in a course, and considered the accuracy and credibility of information from different sources. Measures of internal consistency (alpha reliability) exceed 0.80 for the CCSEQ quality-of-effort scales.

Research on the construct validity of the CCSEQ quality-of-effort scales by Lehman (1992) found that the empirical structure of those scales matched their theoretical structure. Ethington (1996) found that the empirical structure of the quality-of-effort scales was similar, irrespective of the subgroup (males versus females or minority versus majority students) being studied. Based on her findings, Ethington concluded, "Thus, the CCSEQ quality-of-effort scales can be used to provide valid and insightful information for faculty and administrators to use in helping students adapt to the institutional environment and in accommodating the learning needs of particular subgroups of students." In sum, the CCSEQ can be an important component in the assessment programs of two-year institutions interested in evaluating and improving the quantity and quality of student involvement.

References

Ethington, C. A. "An Examination of the Construct Validity of the CCSEQ Quality-of-Effort Scales." *Research in Higher Education, 37*, 1996.

Ewell, P. T., Lovell, C. D., Dressler, P., and Jones, D. P. *A Preliminary Study of the Feasibility and Utility for National Policy of Instructional "Good Practice" Indicators in Undergraduate Education*. NCES 94–437. Washington, D.C.: Government Printing Office, 1994.

Friedlander, J., Murrell, P. H., and MacDougall, P. R. "The Community College Student Experiences Questionnaire." In T. W. Banta and Associates, *Making a Difference: Outcomes of a Decade of Assessment in Higher Education*. San Francisco: Jossey-Bass, 1993.

Lehman, P. W. *CCSEQ: Test Manual and Comparative Data*. Los Angeles: Center for the Study of Evaluation, University of California, 1992.

Pascarella, E. T., and Terenzini, P. T. *How College Affects Students: Findings and Insights from Twenty Years of Research*. San Francisco: Jossey-Bass, 1991.

Gary R. Pike is director of student life studies at the University of Missouri, Columbia.

The Effects of the Cross-Angelo Model of Classroom Assessment on Student Outcomes: A Study

Michelle L. Kalina, Anita Catlin

Classroom assessment techniques can be used in community colleges classes to give teachers valuable feedback on what students are learning. According to the study summarized in this article, these techniques also have other benefits, including improving student involvement and retention. From Assessment Update 6:3.

The Cross-Angelo model of classroom assessment is a teaching method that changes the focus of instruction from an instructor who lectures to students to a shared partnership wherein instructors help students learn and students help instructors teach via the frequent collection of written, anonymous feedback. Anecdotal data indicate that this model has been implemented in many community colleges over the past six years with great success. Both instructors and students seem to like the model. However, the question remains, "Does classroom assessment have an effect on student outcomes?"

We undertook a study to answer this question. The classroom assessment model evaluated in this article is based on Cross's (1988) work on the "classroom/teacher as researcher." Anonymous written feedback from students is handed in and instructors read and respond to the feedback, thereby creating a dialogue with students. Student feedback allows the instructor to alter instruction to meet student needs and gives faculty potent information on which to base instructional decisions. This ongoing anonymous dialogue between student and instructor creates a feedback loop that works to ensure that "what we thought we taught is indeed what students learned."

The College and University Classroom Environment Inventory (CUCEI) (Treagust and Fraser, 1986) was used to assess differences in classroom environments between feedback and no-feedback classes. Treagust and Fraser have done extensive work with college and university students using this instrument, and it has also been used with Australian students who resembled community college students in California.

The current study was conducted under the auspices of a Funds for Instructional Improvement Grant from the California Community College Chancellor's Office. A consortium of eight schools participated. Specifically, the goal was to determine if classroom assessment techniques (CATs) have an effect on five variables: retention rates, final grades and grade distribution, course completion by gender, course completion by ethnicity, and the classroom environment.

A matched-class study was conducted in which instructors who taught two sections of the same course were asked to use feedback techniques in one class and not use them in the other. Comparisons were made between overall retention, grades, student opinion of classroom environment, and course completion by gender and ethnicity. The CUCEI was administered to each section at the end of the tenth week of the semester. The CUCEI was also given to fifteen classes in which the instructor had not been trained in CATs. Data were analyzed using unmatched t-tests, two-way analyses of variance, effect sizes, means, and standard deviations. The results include the following:

1. Retention was increased from 1 percent to 8 percent in CAT or feedback classes, which is consistent with other research findings (Kelly, 1992; Obler, Arnold, Sigala, and Umbdenstock, 1991; Stetson, 1991).

2. There were more A grades and fewer D and F grades in feedback classes than in no-feedback classes.

3. Nine percent more females completed the course in feedback sections. Additionally, on the CUCEI, females differed significantly from males on the overall scores for the inventory and on the personalization, involvement, satisfaction, and individualization subscales.

4. There was no difference in retention between ethnically diverse students and white students. However, there was a clear difference in how ethnically diverse students felt about the classroom environment in classes using feedback methods: their task understanding, cohesiveness, and personalization were significantly enhanced.

5. Students liked the classroom assessment model. They reported more class involvement, cohesiveness, personalization, satisfaction, task understanding, and instructor innovation for feedback classes. Additionally, 98 percent of the faculty who returned a self-report survey said that they liked the model.

6. When CUCEI scores for instructors who used the model were compared with those who had not been trained in the model, statistically significant differences were found on six of the seven subscales and on the compiled score. Additionally, there was an educational effect characterized by a .75 to 1.5 stanine difference on four of the subscales (personalization, involvement, satisfaction, and task) and a 1.0 stanine difference on the compiled score for the feedback group compared with the group in which the instructor had no model training.

The above results led to the following conclusions:

1. Consistent with other research (Kelly, 1992; Obler, Arnold, Sigala, and Umbdenstock, 1991; Stetson, 1991), classroom assessment seems to have a slight, positive effect on retention.

2. Teacher behavior changes when instructors are trained to use the Cross-Angelo classroom assessment model. Since teacher effect is a major determinant of student success, the model may help teachers become more effective.

3. Faculty like using assessment measures with their classes. One of the most difficult parts of this research project was getting faculty to agree to participate in the study. Ironically, this reluctance was due to the fac-

ulty's belief that it was unethical to withhold the model from the test sections because its use had positive effects on instruction, even though there were no quantitative data to support this contention.

4. Grade point average seems to stay the same, but grade distribution is better when classroom assessments are used.

5. Classroom assessment seems to have a positive effect on retention for women in math, science, and technology courses. This is a very heartening finding given that the American Association of University Women (1992) has reported that young women are not being well served in math and science courses.

6. Overall, both past research and our present study indicate that classroom assessment has a positive effect on student outcomes and should be incorporated into teacher training programs in the future.

Our study contributes to an understanding of classroom assessment's effectiveness in terms of measurable student outcomes. Work still needs to be done on the specific effects of CATs on women and ethnically diverse populations, particularly in the math, science, and technology areas. However, this research strongly suggests that classroom assessment methods should be incorporated into teacher training programs, since such techniques have demonstrably positive effects on both student outcomes and faculty.

References

American Association of University Women. *How Schools Shortchange Girls*. Washington, D.C.: AAUW Educational Foundation, 1992.

Cross, K. P. *Feedback in the Classroom: Making Assessments Matter*. Washington, D.C.: American Association of Higher Education, 1988.

Kelly, D. K. *Part-Time and Evening Faculty: Promoting Teaching Excellence for Adult Evening College Students*. Funds for Instructional Improvement Grant Project. Sacramento, Calif.: California Community College Chancellor's Office, 1992.

Obler, S., Arnold, V., Sigala, C., and Umbdenstock, L. "Using Cooperative Learning and Classroom Research for Culturally Diverse Students." In T. A. Angelo (ed.), *Classroom Research: Early Lessons from Success*. New Directions for Teaching and Learning, no. 46. San Francisco: Jossey-Bass, 1991.

Stetson, N. "Implementing and Maintaining a Classroom Research Program for Faculty." In T. A. Angelo (ed.), *Classroom Research: Early Lessons from Success*. New Directions for Teaching and Learning, no. 46. San Francisco: Jossey-Bass, 1991.

Treagust, D. F., and Fraser, B. J. "Validation and Application of the College and University Classroom Environment Inventory (CUCEI)." Paper presented at the 76th annual meeting of the American Educational Research Association, San Francisco, Apr. 1986. (ED 274 692)

Michelle L. Kalina is a faculty member, Humanities division, at Sierra College, Rocklin, California. Anita Catlin is professor of Nursing, Napa Valley College, Napa, California.

Assessing Employer Needs Through the Use of Focus Groups

Sara M. Morris

What are employers looking for from community college graduates? What do they value in employees and what skills are needed? This article describes an approach for gathering this critical information from local employers and using it to inform meaningful changes in stated outcomes for students and the curriculum. From Assessment Update 7:5.

Community colleges that offer one- and two-year technical and vocational programs have a responsibility to keep in touch with the human resources needs of local employers. The effectiveness of individual programs and the college itself depends on their relationship to the local labor market.

Twice in the past seven years, Asheville-Buncombe Technical Community College (A-B Tech) has used focus groups of employers to identify changing entry-level employment needs, as well as to learn of upgrading requirements for current employees. Employers tell the college what they value in their labor forces and why certain skills or abilities are needed. In these productive sessions, employers are candid in revealing what prevents them from hiring people and what the college can do to graduate the most effective employees. They do not hesitate to explain how they think the job of educating people should be done.

The purpose of this article is to describe a process that effectively detects significant trends and issues facing different economic sectors and highlights the broad training and educational needs of community employers. In addition, I explain briefly how results from the process lead program managers and faculty toward meaningful curriculum revisions and updated student outcomes.

Understanding Community Needs

Ample quantitative data are available about the number of jobs in each economic sector and trends relative to growth and decline in employment. Follow-up surveys give colleges answers to questions about placement rates of graduates and about the satisfaction level of employers with entry-level skills of graduates.

Quantitative data, however, do not reveal employers' concerns about trends and issues of the various economic sectors at work in a community. While each A-B Tech curriculum uses an advisory committee of practitioners to help with equipment updates and curriculum changes, these practitioners do not have access to the big picture that resides in the mind of the individual ultimately responsible for the success of the operation.

Process of Assessment

The Asheville-Buncombe community enjoys a diverse economy that revolves around health care, manufacturing, public service, tourism, retail trade, and business and financial services. Once every five years, chief executive officers from each of these sectors are invited to participate in focus groups.

Determining Participants. The key to quality discussions that focus on the future, identify trends, and isolate issues depends upon the position held by the participant. The individual must be from upper-level management: the CEO, plant manager, fire or police chief, hospital administrator, banking executive, mayor, or county commissioner. In our experience, questions addressed to people with vision give the college its best information.

Although groups can range from 8 to 15 participants, the process seems to work best with no fewer than 8 and no more than 10 individuals. In order to keep discussions focused on their needs, the most visible or respected person from each sector is asked to chair discussions. This approach tends to keep the participants on task. Members talk among themselves and become so involved in what they are learning that they forget they are providing planning information for the college. Repeatedly, members talk about how much they gained from the discussion and suggest that they should meet more often.

Handling the Details. All logistical details associated with the effort are worked out by the college. The process allows for either one three-hour meeting or two, two- to three-hour meetings. This decision rests with the chair. Both schedules have been used without any discernible differences in the quality of results.

Prior to the first meeting, participants receive questions to be covered during the discussion. Sample questions from the focus group for manufacturing include the following: Trends in manufacturing? Problems currently facing the manufacturing sector? Where do you see job growth occurring in this sector? What is causing or will cause this demand to occur? Are there major skill deficiencies among the present work force? How do the trends or skill deficiencies affect the need for additional training or education? What can A-B Tech do to help with training needs? What new programs or courses should the college investigate? What skills, beyond technical skills, should graduates of community colleges possess?

Discussions are scheduled around a meal, usually breakfast or lunch. The only college personnel included in this process is the planner, who does not actively participate in the discussion. Limiting participants to individuals from the sector keeps the focus on their needs rather than on the college's need to know.

All discussions are audio recorded. Once a meeting has concluded, tape recordings are fully transcribed as soon as possible. If the chair has decided to hold two sessions, participants are sent transcripts prior to the second meeting. Meeting summaries are returned to participants with the request that they review them to ensure accuracy.

Analyzing the Information. So that the information gleaned from focus groups becomes the property of everyone in the college, members of the president's planning team, rather than the planner, summarize the transcripts. After they have read the comments, members meet to report their analyses and to identify key suggestions and recommendations made by the groups.

Communicating Results. The total college community is invited to a presentation of the findings by focus group chairs. The staff and faculty are given a handout that contains the summary as previously determined by the planning team, a list of all participants by company affiliation and job title, and the discussion questions used by the focus groups along with a few definitive quotes.

Using the Information. The college planning team uses the summary as background for planning assumptions and for writing strategies for its institutional effectiveness plan. In those cases where participants have identified the need for a new training program, the vice president of instruction, division dean, and college planner convene a smaller group made up of practitioners to discuss further the extent of actual need. At this point, the college has been told by top management that a need exists for a new training program or for a better-trained applicant pool. If the practitioners affirm this need, a feasibility study is conducted. Over the years, the college has developed a comprehensive feasibility process that surveys 100 percent of potential employers in the service area.

When a training issue or trend is identified that affects an existing college program, the department chair is given the information and asked to continue the assessment process. The chair and other faculty will interview all focus group participants that represented the program area in addition to eight or ten other key employers. Based on these interviews, a comprehensive survey is designed and administered to 100 percent of the targeted group of employers. Faculty use the information from the survey and interviews to revise student outcomes for the program or to modify the curriculum within the guidelines of statewide curriculum standards, but to the level of need in the local community.

Other Benefits. This process brings key leadership from each of the major employing groups to the campus and acquaints them with college services and programs. Participants are pleased that the institution wants to learn firsthand about their expectations of entry-level employees. These discussions create a renewed awareness of the college as a community partner that shares employers' concerns about the future.

Finally, the college learns to speak the employers' language, which helps when creating messages directed at individual sectors. In the most recent discussions, the manufacturing community referred to its need for people with "soft skills." In the next series of course announcements aimed at employee upgrading, the term *soft skills* was used as a heading for courses in communications, team building, and critical thinking.

Conclusion

While this process may seem to be labor intensive, it has proved to be the most effective way of gathering community-based information that directly affects the college's future and specifically responds to customer needs.

Sara M. Morris is director of development at Asheville-Buncombe Technical Community College, Asheville, North Carolina.

The Butler County Community College Individualized Student Assessment Pilot Project

Phil Speary

How can we understand what individual students are learning? Faculty at Butler County Community College undertook a pilot project to address this chal-

lenge, developing their own approach for using standardized rubrics to measure how well individual students have achieved a range of identifiable outcomes— from ability to engage in teamwork to critical thinking and more. Then they compiled the data from scoring individual students' work to obtain information about curricular strengths and weaknesses. From Assessment Update *14:3.*

Contemporary advances in the assessment of students' achievement of learning outcomes are prompting a reevaluation of the merit of traditional methods of documenting individual student performance. The process of letter grades assigned at the end of a course averaged together to compute a grade point average and printed in chronological sequence to produce a traditional transcript yields no clear information about what exactly a student has achieved in terms of learning outcomes. Letters and aggregate numbers seem to be of more significance than what learning has actually taken place. Potential employers find transcripts of little use because they bear no clear, specific evidence of students' development of desired abilities and skills.

The Learning Outcomes Project

A Community College Strategies column in the November–December 2001 issue of *Assessment Update* documented Butler County Community College's ongoing process of assessing general education outcomes across the curriculum on an aggregate basis. In addition to that effort, Butler County Community College (BCCC) is also participating in the League for Innovation 21st Century Learning Outcomes Project, which began in fall 2000. The 21st Century Learning Outcomes Project involves assessment and documentation of individual students' achievement of learning outcomes that have been identified as crucial for success in the twenty-first century. Out of this piloting process, it is hoped that practical models for such individualized assessment of students at the community college level will emerge.

The BCCC Learning PACT

In spring 2001, members of the Butler Learning Outcomes Project (LOP) Team revised the complex list of learning outcomes it had been employing for several years to form a new compact format called the Butler Learning PACT. PACT is an acronym that represents the major categories of learning outcomes included in the Butler model:

P = Personal Development Skills
- Self-concept
- Health management
- Time management
- Coping with change
- Effective relationships
- Teamwork
- Valuing diversity
- Effective citizenship
- Ethical conduct
- Leadership

A = *Analytical Thinking Skills*
- Problem solving
- Critical thinking
- Historical interpretation
- Aesthetic response

C = *Communication Skills*
- Reading
- Writing
- Listening
- Speaking
- Nonverbal communication

$T = Technological\ Skills$
- Computer literacy
- Internet use
- Field-related technology

The Butler LOP Team is overseeing the piloting of individualized assessment of student achievement in all of these skill areas through activities conducted in representative courses from all discipline areas, augmented by observation and interview processes focusing on various student activity programs. This pilot process will continue over the next several years.

Beginning the Pilot Process

Butler began the pilot process in summer semester 2001 with two courses: Basic Principles of Speech (SP 100) and Substance Abuse Awareness (BS 115). Only selected sections of these courses were involved in the summer pilot, in order to keep the size of the project manageable. Faculty teaching those sections selected the specific Learning PACT outcomes to be assessed. They generated the assessment instruments to be used and the standardized rubrics to score student work for those selected outcomes. In fall 2001, the faculty who had conducted the pilot analyzed both the data and the assessment process and then reported to the LOP Team and other faculty in their discipline areas about the pilot. In spring semester 2002, additional sections of SP 100 and BS 115 that were taught by a broader range of full-time and part-time faculty became involved in the ongoing and revised pilot process.

The Speech Pilot

Two faculty members designed the Basic Principles of Speech individualized assessment process. They agreed that various assignments regularly incorporated into the Basic Principles of Speech class could be used as assessment instruments to evaluate students' achievement of learning outcomes for critical thinking, speaking, listening, and teamwork. These faculty also decided to generate new instruments that would assess students' achievement of learning outcomes for health management, time management, and ethical conduct.

The faculty designated the most advanced informative speech assignment and the most advanced persuasive speech assignment as the assessment instruments for critical thinking and speaking. A standardized rubric was then generated for each of those speeches. The criteria used in those rubrics were taken from the course objectives stated in the recently revised Basic Principles of Speech course outline prepared by Butler speech faculty.

When students presented these two speeches, in addition to assigning traditional grades, the instructors scored students' performances using the standardized rubrics. Students' scores for the two speeches were then translated to the Learning PACT critical thinking and speaking rubrics. Thus students' performances on the two speaking assignments could be used as assessment tools indicating their achievement of critical thinking and speaking learning outcomes.

The two pilot faculty members also agreed to use the graded assignments in the course's listening unit as a means of assessing students' achievement of Learning PACT listening learning outcomes. They designated specific speeches to test students' listening comprehension and critical listening skills. Students' responses to the designated speeches were scored using standardized rubrics for listening comprehension and critical listening, which the two faculty had generated on the basis of the Speech 100 course outcomes for listening. Students' scores on these two rubrics were then translated to the Learning PACT rubric for listening.

A standardized teamwork rubric was used to score students' achievement of outcomes for that Learning PACT skill. The two pilot faculty used group tasks assigned in the course's group discussion and problem-solving unit as the assessment instruments for this learning outcome. The faculty observed students as they worked together in groups and used the rubrics to assess students' behavior. One of the faculty also asked students to use the rubrics to conduct self-assessments.

The faculty also wanted to assess students' achievement in three other personal development areas: health management, time management, and ethical conduct. They created a pair of rubrics for each of these areas. The first in each pair is a self-assessment to be completed by the student at the beginning and the end of the semester. The second is to be used by a faculty member at the end of the semester after having observed the student throughout the course. The health management rubrics focus specifically on stress management and performance anxiety.

As the semester progressed, students completed the various assignments that were being used for assessment. All of the assignments were integrated in the normal coursework. No particular emphasis was given to assignments used for assessment; however, the overall process of assessment was presented at the beginning of the semester. The faculty explained the pilot process to the students, emphasizing its potential benefit to them as a record of their achievement of specific learning skills during their participation in the course.

At the end of the semester, the Butler Office of Assessment gathered the assessment instruments, translated the scores for entry under the Learning PACT rubrics, and recorded the results on the student performance records. The Office of Assessment created a document for each participating student that listed their level of achievement in each assessed learning outcome. Students received hard copies of their individual student performance records by mail. Students taking this speech course received not only a letter grade but also a specific record of what they had accomplished in the course in relation to the Butler Learning PACT outcomes.

This pilot individualized assessment of student performance in speech did more than provide documentation of academic achievement for individual students. The Butler Office of Assessment was able to compile aggregate data from all the scores produced from participating students' work. Thus, the assessment office was able to obtain helpful assessment data profiling students' achievement of learning outcomes in critical thinking, speaking, listening, teamwork, health management, time management, and ethical conduct from one complete set of student work. Assessment data were generated through regular assignments integrated in normal coursework rather than from assessment instruments unrelated to students' coursework.

Growth of the Model

The Butler Individualized Student Assessment Pilot has grown significantly since summer 2001. Instructors of courses ranging from Music Theory to Chemistry I to Graphics I and Statistics for the Social Sciences initiated pilot projects similar to the speech pilot in fall semester 2001. In addition, the BCCC choir embarked on a yearlong study of student learning in personal development skills.

Enthusiasm has spread among faculty to the extent that instructors from eighteen discipline areas are either participating in individualized student assessment pilots in spring semester 2002 or are generating action plans for implementation in fall semester 2002. The faculty overseeing the school's newspaper staff are conducting a study of student learning of personal development skills similar to that being conducted with the choir. The Butler coaching staff and director of residence facilities are working with the Office of Assessment to develop similar studies for the football team and the residence hall assistants to begin in fall 2002. The chemistry faculty have expanded their student assessment portfolio pilot to include students' progress through Chemistry II. Lifetime Fitness instructors are implementing student self-assessment and faculty assessment of health management skills. History instructors are piloting assessment of student achievement in critical thinking, historical interpretation, and effective citizenship. The information technology faculty have initiated a pilot project in cooperation with Brainbench, a testing corporation, to create individual e-transcripts that certify students' achievement of a wide range of computer skills. These are just some of the ways in which the Butler pilot project is growing. One of the most encouraging aspects of the project has been the level

of faculty interest. As faculty see the direct impact of assessment on students, their enthusiasm for assessment of student learning outcomes dra-
matically increases.

Phil Speary is director of assessment at Butler County Community College, El Do-
rado, Kansas.

Assessing Learning Communities

Charles L. Van Middlesworth

*Learning communities are especially challenging to assess because, as the au-
thor points out, they don't "lend themselves to off-the-shelf assessment design."
For that reason, when the faculty at Metropolitan Community College District
in Kansas City began to wonder whether students within a learning community learned as much as students taking the same course through conventional
classroom methods, it was necessary to use a combination of standardized and
faculty-developed approaches. Here is a description of their multimethod approach. From Assessment Update 15:2.*

Learning communities are clusters of courses that are taught as an integrated instructional unit or through linking one course with another. As
a means of instructional delivery, learning communities have increased
in popularity over the past years. This popularity in community colleges
has been notable because as a teaching and learning activity, learning
communities create a form of social integration for students who typically
enroll part-time. The learning community venue allows students the opportunity to spend more time with their peers than do students not enrolled in a learning community. Familiarity with fellow students and
seeing faculty for a series of class periods increase the possibilities for student engagement. The premise for student engagement is establishing a

classroom climate that enables a free-flowing discussion and a reciprocal student-teacher relationship. Manifest within the "climate of engagement" is the use of learning dynamics to engage students in dialogue among themselves as well as with faculty. The social integration associated with learning communities provides community college students with several learning opportunities: first, students experience multiple courses within a specified time period; second, the same cluster of students is enrolled in all of the courses; third, students are able to experience both a skill and a content course through faculty collaboration and presentation of different points of view; and fourth, students engage in collaborative learning through classroom projects.

Learning communities present unique challenges to an institution's assessment program because they do not lend themselves to an off-the-shelf assessment design. Adequate assessment of learning communities requires viewing the initiative through several lenses: instruction; communication; social cohesion or interaction; student and faculty learning; student reflections on their learning; and faculty perceptions of learning activities, support, and instructional atmosphere. Assessing learning communities requires more than using standardized instruments to measure what students know; it also involves developing methodologies to find out how students learn. While most methods used by community colleges involve quantitative measures, learning communities require innovative designs that use qualitative data to expand the assessment and make it more personal for students. One example of personalizing assessment can be seen through a structure and design that "captures student voices" (Tinto, n.d.; Moore, 1998). This method structures student and faculty verbal responses so that comments and observations can be categorized by theme and context. For example, McGregor's work (1991) shows that when students conduct end-of-course self-evaluations, the most frequent outcomes identified are "developing self-esteem and motivation, developing sensitivity and respect for others, building community, making interdisciplinary connections, becoming life-long learners, and building fundamental communication and writing skills" (p. 9).

Merging the Evaluation and Assessment Processes

When the learning community initiative began within the Metropolitan Community College District (MCCD), the primary focus was evaluation of the process rather than assessment of student learning. Of particular interest were faculty and student satisfaction; retention; and comparison of grade-point averages for learning community students and non–learning community students. We concentrated on the effectiveness of the delivery system, faculty adjustment to a team teaching approach, and student response to being an active as opposed to a passive learner. But faculty wondered whether students within a learning community learned as much as students taking the same course through conventional classroom methods. Thus it was necessary to develop multiple levels of evaluation and learning assessment. The multiple methodologies that were implemented included both quantitative and qualitative data collection and analysis.

Many learning communities faculty were concerned that current standardized assessment instruments failed to adequately capture the influence of the learning community pedagogy on student learning. The transition from evaluating the learning community initiative to assessing student learning required a major shift in emphasis. It was necessary to view not only what students learn but also how they go about learning. For faculty, the shift to examining how students learn became the link between the general education assessment program and student learning within learning communities.

Methodologies

The variety of methods used in the MCCD to assess learning communities is the result of several years of analyzing institutional data. It was clear that faculty who were teaching in learning communities did not want intrusive assessment; instead, they wanted assessment that provided information about how their students learn. Gradually, assessment components were added to answer questions about student learning as well as instructional delivery. Letting these teaching and learning information needs develop gradually did much to ensure the acceptance and adoption of the following assessment methodologies.

The assessment design for learning communities includes six methods that are both quantitative and qualitative: (1) structured interviews of students and faculty, (2) classroom observation, (3) a student learning survey, (4) embedded course assessment, (5) norm-referenced instruments, and (6) the Measure of Intellectual Development. The foundation for the qualitative methodologies is the "captured voice" model introduced by Moore (1998). This model includes seven attributes: (1) writing/thinking/argumentation; (2) application/transfer of learning; (3) teamwork/group skills; (4) active agent in learning/developing a voice; (5) collaboration and development of empathy for "other"; (6) connection making; and (7) understanding context/developing perspective. *Writing/thinking/argumentation* refers to critical thinking skills and a student's ability to engage in dialogue and see diverse ways of dealing with the same issue, subject, or content. *Application/transfer of learning* refers to how or if students can apply or transfer their learning to events or situations outside the classroom. *Teamwork/group skills* requires evidence of a student's ability to work effectively in groups to produce or create a product or report. Being an *active agent in learning/developing a voice* refers to students' comfort level in a course, feeling they are a part of the class through participation, and the response they receive from others. *Collaboration and development of empathy for "other"* refers to a student's ability to work with others and recognize others for their cooperation or opinions. *Connection making* refers to finding links with topics and issues in class and with those in the greater world or on the job. *Understanding context/developing perspective* involves understanding discipline-based issues and assumptions, which enables students to develop their own perspective on an issue or to accept one that exists outside their personal comfort level (Moore, 1998).

Structured Interviews. The structured student interview has been used in the MCCD since 1997 for gathering student impressions of their learning community experiences. The structured student interview is a means for acquiring student reflections on their experience with a learning community. Question content varies from "Why did you choose a learning community?" to changes a student would make regarding how the course was offered to several probing questions about their experiences within the community. Direct questioning is avoided in order to afford students the opportunity to describe the experiences of using collaboration as a learning technique, developing empathy for others, or understanding the context of a multidisciplinary explanation. The ability of students to describe their learning experiences provides the learning communities steering committee with evidence that students are making connections.

The structured faculty interview is used to query faculty about their experiences with learning communities as a delivery system. Of particular interest is how the learning community format can be used in each discipline. The faculty model, like that for the student interview, uses Moore's seven captured voice model attributes to categorize responses to questions. Faculty engaged in learning communities on a consistent basis report that the experience has rejuvenated them as classroom teachers. Faculty serving on a teaching team with colleagues from different disciplines have an opportunity to engage students in learning through discussions at multiple levels, including faculty-to-faculty, faculty-to-student, and student-to-student.

Classroom Observation. Another methodology involves using observation to examine such classroom dynamics as students interacting with a guest lecturer, deciding which group to join, workload distribution within a group, dealing with group work and group grade, and interacting with group members with whom they disagree. The observation process provides evidence of how students and faculty interact to facilitate the workflow and how students learn. Observational data, like those from the structured interview format, are analyzed and categorized according to the captured voice model.

Student Learning Survey. A student learning survey is administered as students enter and exit a learning community. Survey items were constructed based on information acquired from the structured student interviews and classroom observations. Students are asked to indicate the degree to which specific learning activities or events occurred in class—for example, "When examining complex problems, I enjoy the diverse viewpoints that different courses can provide on the same topic" or "I enjoy discussing issues with people who don't agree with me." The survey follows Moore's captured voice model, which provides the framework for the learning communities initiative. The survey links structured interviews and classroom observations to evaluate student learning.

Course-Embedded Assessment. Course-embedded assessment is used to test institutional general education student outcomes. Faculty identify student outcomes within their courses that can be connected to one of the institution's eight general education components. For instance, some of the attributes for critical thinking have been met by incorporating them in a history assignment. The history assignment is designed to assess a student's use of the methods of inquiry of history and the social sciences to evaluate problems. This assignment accomplishes several things: first, it meets one of the course requirements; second, it assesses several critical thinking attributes; and third, it assesses an attribute of the "Awareness of the Social, Political and Economic Environment" general education component.

Faculty use grading rubrics to determine competence levels for course content and for each general education requirement. Course-embedded assessment has been an effective way to move faculty from thinking that assessing students is simply providing them with a course grade to using assessment to identify how well student learning outcomes are met.

Nationally Normed Instruments. Standardized, norm-referenced instruments are used to assess a student's knowledge in regard to specific general education outcomes. Faculty believe that no one standardized instrument is sufficient to measure all aspects of a general education component such as communication or critical thinking, so standardized or norm-referenced instruments are often more acceptable when used in conjunction with locally developed assessments of student learning. Standardized or norm-referenced instruments are most often used as a starting point or a means of benchmarking a general education component or attribute.

Measure of Intellectual Development (MID). The Measure of Intellectual Development is popular within the learning communities movement. The MID is a production-style essay that has been used extensively in assessing student learning and evaluating educational experiences. Advocates claim it to be a good measure of the learning goals in collaborative learning environments. The MID has been found to be most effective when it is administered in class or in a standardized setting. It can be administered as a take-home assignment, but because this provides no control on time, it is difficult to ensure that students take the necessary time to do well. Greater benefit is obtained from the MID when students have a reasonable level of basic writing skill and are able to articulate their cognition. Deficiencies in writing skills can produce responses that make the MID very difficult to rate. The most significant limitation of the MID is that it must be sent outside the institution for scoring and rating, making it somewhat expensive.

Program Improvement Through Process Evaluation and Learning Assessment

Learning communities are dynamic instructional environments that require constant feedback to be effective. The feedback that is available for faculty review is both formative and summative. Instructional teams have frequent meetings to ensure that students are obtaining the appropriate cognitive information and that the learning environment and activities create a climate that is conducive to learning. Faculty engage in a post-semester review of instructional activities to check on whether teaching and learning outcomes were met. In addition, a learning communities steering committee, as well as faculty from the communities, meet for a review of all assessment and evaluative data produced and to discuss changes that should be implemented for the following semester.

References

McGregor, J. "What Difference Do Learning Communities Make?" *Washington Center News*, 1991, 6(1), 4–9.

Moore, W. S. "Exploding Minds and Other Hazards of 'Really Learning': Assessing and Promoting Student and Faculty Learning in Learning Communities." National Learning Communities Dissemination Project Institute, Washington Center for Undergraduate Education, Olympia, July 26, 1998.

Tinto, V. "Building Learning Communities for New College Students: A Summary of Research Findings of the Collaborative Learning Project." Utica, N.Y.: National Center on Postsecondary Teaching, Learning and Assessment, Syracuse University, n.d.

Charles L. Van Middlesworth is director of research, evaluation, and assessment for the Metropolitan Community Colleges, Kansas City, Missouri.

Assessing Additional Elements of the Community College Mission

A New Paradigm for Evaluating
Transfer Success

Michael Quanty, Richard Dixon, Dennis Ridley

After an assessment team from Thomas Nelson Community College and Christopher Newport University had analyzed student transfer success from every conceivable angle, they were surprised and frustrated that they had come up with no findings that could be translated into concrete recommendations for improvement. They went back to the drawing board and came up with the Course-Based Model of Transfer Success, an easy-to-implement evaluation model that can provide faculty at both the sending and receiving colleges with comprehensive and relevant information about student transfer success. From Assessment Update 10:2.

Thomas Nelson Community College (TNCC) and Christopher Newport University (CNU) have been trying to improve transfer success rates for years. In 1989, with support from the State Council for Higher Education in Virginia's Funds for Excellence program, we set out to establish a new standard in transfer research. Reasoning that the key to improving transfer is faculty involvement, we reassigned time for two faculty members from each college to review data, design follow-up studies, and then make recommendations to improve the process. For a full year the faculty and research staffs pored over a variety of analyses and a plethora of data. Using detailed records for more than 1,800 students who transferred, we created regression analyses predicting grade-point average at CNU; profiled successful and unsuccessful transfer students; and explored the effects of hours attempted and completed at TNCC, degree type, courses taken, and every conceivable demographic variable. We also employed a consultant to interview students regarding their experience at the colleges.

At the end of the year, we had uncovered a number of statistically significant findings. However, when it came to making recommendations we were at a loss. Even though we had examined students' success from every angle we could imagine and spent hours discussing the data, we had no idea what should be done. Knowing that women and older students experience less "transfer shock" provides little basis for action. Faculty cannot change students' demographic backgrounds. They also cannot make students complete at least thirty hours before transferring.

In the aftermath of this frustration, however, we experienced an epiphany; we made a paradigm shift. The result is the Course-Based Model of Transfer Success (CBMTS), a new model for evaluating transfer that we maintain can greatly enhance the ability of the nation's community colleges and four-year colleges and universities to improve the success of transfer students. It provides faculty with action-oriented results they can use to improve students' preparation. The basic difference between this new model and those commonly employed in transfer research is that it is course-based rather than student-based.

This shift is simple but crucial. Whereas traditional research tracks particular *students* from the community college to their transfer institution, the CBMTS yields information that shows how well students who complete course prerequisites at a community college perform in specific *courses* compared to students who complete the prerequisites at the receiving college. The emphasis is on how well courses prepare students. This pinpoints for faculty exactly where students experience difficulty. It also creates a sense of urgency. Faculty agree that students who pass their course are prepared for subsequent courses which require that course as a prerequisite.

CBMTS is simple and relatively easy to implement, and provides comprehensive data that are immediately and obviously relevant to faculty at both the sending and receiving college. In short, it provides useful information. We developed a tracking system that examines every course having a prerequisite that could be met at CNU, TNCC, or at another college. For each course so identified, the program provides a grade distribution for students, broken out by semester and by whether the prerequisite was taken at CNU, at TNCC, or at another institution. A summary for each course totals grades across all semesters, and a discipline summary totals grades of all courses in the discipline and then for all semesters included. Chi-square analysis determines whether any observed differences are statistically significant. We now have data from spring 1990 through spring 1997 for TNCC and CNU.

The results we have obtained thus far are very encouraging for community colleges. Generally, we have found that students who complete course prerequisites at TNCC perform at a level at least equivalent to students who complete prerequisites at CNU. The real strength of our new model is that when a problem is identified it can be attributed to a specific course at the community college and at the receiving college. Faculty take ownership for students who have successfully completed their course(s). If those students are not prepared for subsequent coursework, faculty want to know why. Demographic considerations do not matter when a faculty member has certified that the student has mastered course requirements.

This paradigm also works well within a total quality or customer service orientation. The receiving institution and the transferring institution have a customer-supplier partnership with shared interest in students' success. Identifying course-specific deficiencies allows quick and continuous improvements to be implemented and tested.

In October 1996 the Fund for the Improvement of Postsecondary Education (FIPSE) awarded us a grant to develop a "generic" version of CBMTS that can be adapted to support other college partnerships. Currently we are working with most of the community colleges and four-year colleges and universities in Virginia to develop and test a program that will give course-based comparisons using data that are collected centrally by a state council (a number of other states have similar arrangements). The information required to run the model can be produced easily by most colleges even without centralized reporting. Partners need to be able to share three types of files: (1) course files that include a student identifier, course identifier, course grade, and term (one record per student per course); (2) a target-course file that lists all courses at the four-year college or university that have prerequisites; and (3) a course-equivalency file that identifies community college courses that transfer as prerequisites for particular target courses.

With these basic files and a commitment to improvement, colleges can begin examining transfer in an exciting new way. Our experience at both TNCC and CNU has shown that faculty respond positively to the information generated by the model. When a problem is found, faculty talk to one another and find a solution. We also have found the model useful in a number of other applications. CNU, for example, uses it as one means of assessing the effectiveness of courses delivered on-line. They determined that students who complete courses on-line perform comparably to traditional students in follow-on courses. In fact, once we saw the power of the model, we began to use it in many contexts. It works; it gives faculty data that are both useful and motivating.

Through FIPSE support, we will be helping other colleges adopt CBMTS and customize it to their specifications. If you would like to learn more about the model, we encourage you to contact one of us directly or to visit our Web site at <http://www.cnu.edu/cbmts>.

Michael Quanty and Richard Dixon are at Thomas Nelson Community College. Dennis Ridley is at Christopher Newport University.

Corporate Partnership Student Assessment: The Owens Community College Experience

David H. Devier

Effective vocational and technical education often depends on the success of educational partnerships between community colleges and local employers. This article details how one college approaches the task of assessing the outcomes that emerge from student experiences in such partnerships. From Assessment Update *14:5.*

Owens Community College is a comprehensive community college with two campuses, one in Perrysburg and the other in Findlay, Ohio. Total enrollment exceeds 17,000 students, and the majority of students attend the Perrysburg campus. Programs range from traditional occupational-technical offerings in health, public services, business, and industrial and engineering technologies to transfer Associate of Arts and Associate of Science degrees to workforce and community education.

Owens Community College, like most institutions of higher education, has been focused on student assessment for some time. As part of an ongoing assessment process, the Industrial and Engineering Technologies (IET) Division has developed workable, effective assessment models. This report discusses the Owens IET corporate partnership programs and the student assessment models used to determine the outcomes of these programs and guide improvements.

Within the Industrial and Engineering Technologies Division, there are four academic departments: design technologies, manufacturing and industrial operations technologies, electrical/electronics engineering technologies, and transportation technologies. Most of the corporate partnerships have been developed by the Transportation Technologies Department and include the Ford Motor Company Automotive Student Service Educational Training (ASSET) option, the General Motors Corporation Automotive Service Educational Program (ASEP) option, the John Deere Agricultural Technician option, the Caterpillar Dealer Service Technician Program option, and the Cooperative Automotive Service Technician (CAST) option. All of these, with the exception of the CAST option, are national programs with multiple sites at various colleges around the United States. Most of these programs have similar program assessment processes. The CAST option uses assessment approaches similar to the others, but because it is one of a kind, its assessment process has unique traits. All five programs lead to an Associate of Applied Science degree and use the same general education assessment methods. The general education program, as well as the models for the corporate programs' major skill sets, will be outlined later in this article. In addition to the transportation technologies corporate partnerships, one additional partnership, the Cisco Wide Area Networking Technology program, is housed in the Electrical/Electronics Engineering Technologies Department and is associated with a regional Cisco Academy.

Outlines of Corporate Partnership Programs

Two automotive corporate partnerships (ASSET and ASEP) are patterned after the basic automotive program, with skill courses that are specialized by make of vehicle studied and worked on in the laboratory. Both Ford and General Motors donate vehicles for use in the courses; in turn, Owens donates some of these vehicles to local high schools. The CAST option uses the standard automotive courses, with technical field experiences at local nonbrand repair shops such as BP ProCare and Tireman, Inc. The ASSET and ASEP options use technical field experiences at local Ford-Lincoln-Mercury or General Motors dealerships.

The curriculum of the John Deere option is a version of the diesel program that is specialized by brand, with technical field experience offered at regional John Deere dealerships. The Caterpillar Dealer Service Technician Program is patterned after the Think Big program that was developed by Caterpillar Corporation to establish college programs across the country. Because the program varies considerably from the diesel program, it had to be approved by the Ohio Board of Regents as a stand-alone program.

General Education Assessment

The general education components of all of the corporate partnership programs are identical. These course-based components include Composition I and II, Small Group Communication, College Algebra, Trigonometry I and II, and Fundamentals of Computer Systems. Assessment of general education is collegewide and currently takes place in each course and at degree completion. Measures are applied in randomly selected sections of each of these courses. The measures include pretests and posttests, as well as writing samples in the composition courses and speech evaluations in the oral communication course. The American College Testing's Collegiate Assessment of Academic Proficiency (ACT-CAAP) is administered to a random sample of graduating students each year to determine students' exit-level knowledge and skills in English composition, college math, and personal communication. Basic computer skill is currently measured only at the course level.

Assessment of Corporate Partnership Student Skills

Assessment of the program-level skills and knowledge required by the corporate partnerships is a multifaceted process. Each program has a mission statement that is directly related to the division's mission, which in turn is derived from the Owens mission. The mission sets the stage for the development of program goals and student learning outcome objectives. To evaluate student success in achieving the outcomes, faculty members choose specific assessments and record the number of students passing each on computer spreadsheets throughout the two-year curriculum. All sections of courses are included in this process. Each semester, the appropriate faculty members receive a letter requesting these data and a form on which to report the data to the department chair. Students are also evaluated by technical field experience supervisors as an external measure of their learning.

The chair analyzes the data each semester and reports the results to the faculty, the appropriate advisory committee, and the College Assessment Committee. These bodies conduct additional reviews of the data and recommend adjustments in curriculum, objectives, or measures as needed. Examples of the purpose statements, student outcome statements, and data reporting form for the Caterpillar Dealer Service Technician program are shown in Exhibits 1 and 2.

The result of this process for each partnership program is the generation of data that speak to each outlined student outcome. These data are used to determine how the program is doing and what, if any, changes need to be made either in the program or in the assessment process itself.

Owens Community College, like all educational institutions, is struggling with the assessment of student learning. Assessment of the corporate partnerships at Owens is unique only in terms of the specific skill areas related to given product lines—John Deere, Ford, and so on. The general approach of using course-embedded assessment, external reviews

Exhibit 1. Student Outcomes for Transportation Technologies–Caterpillar Dealer Service Technician Program

Purpose Statements	Student Outcome Statements
1. Students will understand the operation of air conditioning systems.	1a. Students will be familiar with air conditioning service operations.
2. Students will diagnose electronic systems.	2a. Students will read wiring diagrams to explain electrical circuit operation. 2b. Students will use test meters to diagnose electrical circuits.
3. Students will understand engine operation and repair.	3a. Students will disassemble, inspect, and reassemble diesel engines.
4. Students will understand driveline operations, including power-shift transmission and torque converters.	4a. Students will be able to disassemble and reassemble driveline components. 4b. Students will explain power-shift transmission operation.
5. Students will understand conventional diesel fuel systems and computerized fuel injection systems.	5a. Students will utilize diagnostic tools to diagnose and repair fuel systems.
6. Students will service and repair brake systems.	6a. Students will be able to disassemble and inspect brake system components.
7. Students will understand track and undercarriage operation and adjustments.	7a. Students will be able to adjust tracks and undercarriage.

Exhibit 2. Outcomes Assessment Program for Transportation Technologies–Caterpillar Dealer Service Technician Program

CAT1: Students will understand the operation of air conditioning systems.
CAT1A1:
Outcome: Students will be familiar with air conditioning service operations.
Assessment Tool: CAT 115, Air Conditioning. Students will research and write a paper on Mobile Refrigeration, which will include graphics and a bibliography. The paper will be graded for content.

Response	Met	Action

CAT1A2:
Outcome: Students will be familiar with air conditioning service operations.
Assessment Tool: CAT 115, Air Conditioning. Students will complete the ASE Refrigerant Recovery and Recycling Review and Quiz, which may be mailed in to obtain ASE certification.

Response	Met	Action

CAT1A3:
Outcome: Students will be familiar with air conditioning service operations.
Assessment Tool: CAT 115, Air Conditioning. Students will complete the Liquid/Vapor written test.

Response	Met	Action

via field experience evaluations, and the CAAP exam at graduation is effective in establishing a database through which to gauge student learning in all the corporate programs. Continued refinement of the process is
key to ensuring that the assessment of student learning is of real value for
both program validation and program improvement.

David H. Devier is dean of University of Cincinnati Clermont College, and formerly
dean of industrial and engineering technologies at Owens Community College.

Closing the Feedback Loop: How an Outcomes Assessment Instrument Has Led to Positive Curricular Reform

Diane K. Chaddock

*One of the biggest challenges for community colleges is to graduate students
who know how to write. While most faculty have a lot of experience assessing
writing skills, as the faculty at Southwestern Michigan College discovered, struc-
turing assessments that improve the teaching of writing is more complicated.
The author describes an approach that helped faculty identify and begin to address an important gap between the skills students acquired in developmental
composition and those needed for success in more advanced courses. From Assessment Update 12:3.*

Nearly all colleges and universities in the nation are involved to some
extent in the development and implementation of some type of academic outcomes assessment strategy. For many, these strategies have not been
in place long enough to determine whether they can actually lead to curricular improvement and increased student learning. At Southwestern
Michigan College, one such academic outcomes assessment strategy has
produced faculty-led initiatives to revise and improve instruction in English composition.

Southwestern Michigan College is a rural, comprehensive community college in the southwestern corner of Michigan, serving about 1,800 full-time equivalent students. Since its inception in 1964, the college has regularly evaluated its programs and student learning, but in the early 1990s the need for a formal, clearly defined plan for measuring academic outcomes was recognized. During the 1993–94 academic year, faculty presented specific proposals on how to assess academic outcomes. These proposals were then pilot-tested during the 1994–95 academic year. Among the earliest measures of academic outcomes implemented by the college was the English Proficiency Examination.

Measuring Outcomes with the English Proficiency Examination

One of the core competence requirements for all students graduating with an associate degree at Southwestern Michigan College is in writing. This core requirement states, "Upon completion of an Associate Degree at Southwestern Michigan College, a student will organize, select, and relate ideas; outline and develop them in coherent paragraphs; write standard English sentences; use correct spelling and punctuation; achieve a varied writing style including vocabulary and sentence structure for different readers and purposes." In order to master these and other skills, students in a degree program must take two semesters of English composition. In the first course of this sequence, ENGL 103, students learn the core skills described above. All students must place into this course either by achieving a minimal score on the college's Basic Skills Assessment Test or as a result of adequate ACT scores. Students whose test scores indicate that they are not prepared to enter ENGL 103 are placed at the appropriate level in the college's developmental English course sequence. Students may not progress to their second-semester English composition course until they have passed ENGL 103 with a grade of C or better. Now, as part of our outcomes assessment plan, students must also pass the English Proficiency Examination in order to pass the ENGL 103 course.

Since the 1993–94 academic year, the English Proficiency Examination has been administered twice each academic term. Just past the midway point of the semester, students in ENGL 103 are given the one-hour writing proficiency test. In this test, students select from several writing topics, unknown to them until they see the test. Each student's writing sample is then evaluated by three English composition instructors, none of whom may be the student's current instructor. Based on the core writing outcomes described earlier, each student's writing sample must be judged as demonstrating proficiency in these skills by at least two of the three evaluators. Students who fail to pass this examination are counseled by their instructors regarding the areas of weakness identified by the graders and are given one additional opportunity to take the exam. Any student who does not pass the exam after the second attempt will not receive a passing grade in ENGL 103 and must retake the course.

Evaluating Results

Results from the English Proficiency Examination process are evaluated each year by the English Committee, which is composed of faculty from the Communications Department. Evaluation of these results has shown that while at least 90 percent of the students taking the English Proficiency Examination are able to pass, most of those who fail come into ENGL 103 from the developmental English course. English faculty from both the Communications Department and the Developmental Studies Department, along with college administration, have agreed that this is an unacceptable finding.

This was not our only concern, however. Another matter that faculty had to confront was that for many students, the focus on preparation for the proficiency exam that was normally a part of their ENGL 103 course was unnecessary and redundant and kept them from receiving the higher level of instruction for which they were prepared.

Using Results to Improve Curriculum

In Spring 1999, an outside facilitator was brought to the college to facilitate a two-day workshop involving English composition faculty from the

Communications Department and the Developmental Studies Department. One of the primary goals of this workshop was to identify, level, and validate the skills being taught in each English composition course, including those in the developmental sequence. This was considered essential if we were to provide a seamless transition from one course to the next and to prepare students properly for the workplace or for their transfer program. A second goal was to determine if the current English Proficiency Examination, as it was being administered, was the appropriate outcomes assessment instrument at the proper time in the composition sequence.

All full-time English composition faculty participated in the workshop. At the end of the two days, the participants submitted to the administration a comprehensive plan for revision of the English composition sequence. This plan included the following:

- Evaluation of the current English composition placement and matriculation process
- Identification and validation of exit competencies for each of the composition courses
- Leveling of competencies in each course and development of mechanisms for remediation of students with deficient skills
- Replacement of the English Proficiency Examination with periodic measures of outcomes throughout the entire English composition sequence, including an exit examination for the developmental English course and portfolio reviews in all college-level English courses

The process of fully developing and implementing this plan has only begun, and it will continue with a second workshop in spring of 2000. However, significant strides in improving both the curriculum and the assessment process have already been made. The English Proficiency Examination at Southwestern Michigan College is only one measure of academic outcomes assessment. Yet, by assuring that this measure is consistently applied and results are continually analyzed by the individuals responsible for curricular improvement, future students will benefit from better instruction and support for developing the writing outcomes determined to be essential for all graduates. In addition to providing a mechanism for curricular evaluation and improvement, the feedback loop applied to this outcomes assessment measure has allowed college faculty and staff to evaluate and adjust the application of the measure itself.

Diane K. Chaddock is dean of arts and sciences at Southwestern Michigan College.

Assessing Institutional Effectiveness

A Glimpse of Community and Technical College Students' Perceptions of Student Engagement

Judith A. Ouimet

For a number of years the National Survey of Student Engagement has been providing four-year institutions with information on levels of student engagement in and satisfaction with their educational experience. Now there is a similar instrument for community colleges—the Community College Survey of Student Engagement (CCSSE). Findings from a 2002 pilot test of the CCSSE are summarized here. From Assessment Update 15:1.

Student engagement. Is it important for two-year postsecondary institutions to seek information from their students on effective educational practices? Absolutely. Why? According to the 1999 *Digest of Education Statistics*, 45 percent of all first-time freshmen enrolled in degree-granting institutions attended either a public or private two-year college. Approximately 63 percent of students with freshman standing in U.S. higher education institutions attend a community college (*Digest of Education Statistics*, 1999). Since so many students begin there, it is vital that community and technical colleges become proactive in assessing not only the first-year experience on their campuses but also the experiences of all students, whatever their educational goals might be.

A relatively new survey instrument, designed specifically for community and technical colleges, was recently field-tested at 48 U.S. colleges, collecting over 33,000 completed surveys (see Table 1). The Community College Survey of Student Engagement (CCSSE—pronounced "sessie") provides a new focus on educational practices that research shows are related to student success. CCSSE is the "daughter" of the National Survey of Student Engagement (NSSE), headquartered at Indiana University and directed by George Kuh. The CCSSE project is supported by grants from The Pew Charitable Trusts and the Lumina Foundation for Education and is directed by Kay McClenney at the University of Texas at Austin.

CCSSE is a nationally administered in-class survey, with a sampling methodology that allows colleges to compare their findings with those of other participating colleges. The third-party sampling approach provides the randomness necessary for the use of inferential statistics. Target sample sizes are determined by each institution's fall enrollment figures as reported to the Integrated Postsecondary Education Data System (IPEDS), providing the statistical power to do cross-comparisons.

For the field test administration, CCSSE had a target number of respondents for each college. To assist the colleges in obtaining the targeted response numbers, CCSSE provided each college with randomly selected supplemental courses with numbers adjusted for student absenteeism and cancelled classes. As a result, six colleges actually surpassed their targeted number of responses.

Table 1. Sample Size Targets for CCSSE Field Test, 2002

Field Test Groups, by Total Enrollment	Actual	Targeted	Percent of Target
Small colleges (less than 3,000)	7,050	8,625	81.7%
Medium colleges (3,000–7,999)	12,007	14,350	83.7
Large colleges (more than 8,000)	14,460	16,875	85.7
All field test colleges	33,517	39,850	84.1

Profile of CCSSE 2002 Field Test Respondents

When collecting data from students or any other population, respondents should be compared to the underlying population to check the representativeness of the sample. Of the 33,517 respondents, 40.5 percent were male and 59.5 percent female. This reflects the population of community college students, which is 42.9 percent male and 57.1 percent female. Overall, black and white students were underrepresented by 1.3 percent and 6.8 percent respectively, while Native American and international students were overrepresented by 1.8 percent and 5.7 percent respectively. Approximately 65 percent of the respondents reported attending their community college full-time, while approximately 36 percent of the colleges' total student population actually attended full-time. Only 35 percent of the surveyed students reported being part-time college students, compared to 64 percent as reported to IPEDS. This inverse representation is a result of the sampling stratification employed for identifying the day and evening classes selected. Other than enrollment status, the respondents reflect the underlying population at the 48 participating community and technical colleges.

Research tells us that first-generation students are more at risk of dropping out of college than students whose parents are college graduates (Wild and Ebbers, 2002). Of the CCSSE respondents, 21 percent of the students reported that their mother held at least a bachelor's degree, while 27 percent reported that their father had at least a bachelor's degree. Slightly more than a quarter reported that either their mother or father has only a high school degree. When asked about their own education level, 77 percent of all respondents reported that they had earned either a high school diploma or a GED, while 15 percent reported either a vocational certificate or an associate degree. Five percent have a bachelor's degree and 2 percent reported a master's, doctoral, or professional degree.

Some 65 percent of the respondents started their college career at the community college they are presently attending. This is critical information for colleges to have when designing orientation programs, learning communities, or first-year programs aimed at creating an environment that promotes student learning and involvement, especially for first-generation students.

Community colleges have many missions and goals, as do their students. Students were given the opportunity to mark "primary goal," "secondary goal," or "not a goal" in response to a list of possible goals for attending their particular college. Many students marked more than one primary goal. The most popular reason for attending community college was to obtain a degree or certificate, followed by pursuit of additional knowledge and skills. Overall, 61 percent of the students reported that one of their primary goals was to transfer to a four-year college or university; 57 percent wanted to obtain knowledge in a specific area, 56 percent to obtain an associate degree; and 52 percent to obtain job-related skills. Other primary goals were to complete a certificate program (31 percent), to update job skills (27 percent), to change careers (22 percent), and to take one or more courses for self-improvement (22 percent).

An important factor in student success and retention is satisfaction. We know that students who report high levels of satisfaction are more likely to persist and achieve their goals, however those goals may be defined by the student. For this reason, researchers often use student satisfaction as a correlate of retention. A proxy for satisfaction is whether a person recommends a service or institution to others. The CCSSE questionnaire asks students if they would recommend their college to a friend or family member. Ninety-four percent reported that they would make such a recommendation.

Another item asks students to evaluate their entire educational experience—61 percent described their experience as excellent, 25 percent as good, 13 percent as fair, and only 1 percent thought their experience was poor.

Another measure of student satisfaction is the percentage of returning or successful students. Seventy-two percent of the students said they would return for either the summer or fall 2002 quarter or semester, while 9 percent reported that they had achieved their goals and would not be returning. Only 15 percent reported that they were uncertain or had no plans to return.

Are community and technical college students actively involved in their education? It depends. CCSSE recommends collapsing the response categories "often" and "very often" to report levels of engagement, then setting 50 percent of the students participating in an activity as the criterion for assessing levels of engagement. Students reported being engaged most frequently in the following activities:

- Working on a paper or project that required integrating ideas or information from various sources (63 percent)
- Asking questions in class or contributing to class discussions (60 percent)
- Receiving prompt feedback (written or oral) from instructors on class performance (55 percent)
- Discussing ideas from class or class readings with others outside of class (for example, students, family members, coworkers) (54 percent)
- Preparing two or more drafts of a paper or assignment before turning it in (53 percent)

In comparison, it is important to note what students are not doing in college as frequently as one might expect. To gauge the activities that students engaged in least frequently, CCSSE used only the "never" response category. The list of items reported includes those for which at least 30 percent of the students said they never engaged in that activity. These items were as follows:

- Participated in community-based projects as a part of a regular course (76 percent)
- Worked with instructors on activities other than coursework (69 percent)
- Tutored or taught other students (paid or voluntary) (67 percent)
- Discussed ideas from readings or classes with instructors outside of class (44 percent)
- Worked with classmates outside of class to prepare class assignments (36 percent)
- Used an electronic medium (for example, listserv, chat group, Internet) to discuss or complete an assignment (36 percent)

- Used e-mail to communicate with an instructor (32 percent)
- Talked about career plans with an instructor or adviser (30 percent)

In general, community and technical college students reported being somewhat engaged in their coursework. Students are preparing drafts, integrating ideas from various sources, and discussing readings with others outside class. They ask questions or contribute to class discussion and report receiving prompt feedback from their instructors. On the other hand, they are not interacting much with faculty outside class, nor are they collaborating much with other students outside class. Because the vast majority of community colleges are commuter institutions, and because they serve large numbers of part-time students who juggle college with work and family responsibilities, there are clear challenges that must be addressed. Primary among these is how to optimize the use of classroom time by creating an array of opportunities for students to engage with one another, with faculty, and with the subject matter at hand. Finding ways that students can communicate substantively with their peers and faculty outside the classroom setting is also a major challenge.

Using the findings from CCSSE, participating colleges can identify areas where they are performing well and areas where they have opportunities for growth. Colleges can use the results to create initiatives with which to enhance the learning environment for students on campus, to encourage faculty to incorporate more active and collaborative pedagogical techniques in their classes, to provide services that students say are important to their success, and to communicate their successes in student engagement to the college community.

References

Digest of Education Statistics, 1999. National Center for Education Statistics. http://nces.ed.gov/programs/digest.

Wild, L., and Ebbers, L. "Rethinking Student Retention in Community Colleges." *Community College Journal of Research and Practice*, 2002, *26*, 503–519.

Judith A. Ouimet is associate director and project manager of the Community College Survey of Student Engagement at the University of Texas at Austin.

Has the Time Come for National Benchmarking for Community Colleges?

Jeffrey A. Seybert

The author describes two national benchmarking initiatives designed to help community colleges compare their practices, outcomes, and productivity measures with those of peer institutions. One initiative focuses on collecting data related to instructional costs and productivity; the other involves developing a national database that will be accessible to any community college willing to share relevant information on a variety of instructional outcomes, continuing education, workforce development, and other core activities. From Assessment Update 15:3.

As we all know, within the last two decades, higher education has come under increased pressure to become more accountable to the public. Zemsky and Massy (1990), in an important article in *Change* magazine, contend that higher education institutions have reduced faculty teaching and advising loads in favor of other nonteaching, non–student-centered activity to the point where "Undergraduates are paying more to attend institutions in which they receive less attention than in past decades." Henry Rosovsky (1992), former dean of the faculty of arts and sciences at Harvard University, argues that faculty, when viewed as a social organism, operate "without a constitution and with very little common law. That is a poor combination, especially when there is no consensus concerning duties or standards of behavior. This situation has been made infinitely worse by the lack of information in the hands of academic deans." Criticism of higher education is not limited to articles in scholarly publications. The editors of *U.S. News and World Report*, in their 1996 "America's Best Colleges" article, contend that faculty are a major factor in escalating tuition: "Rarely mentioned are the on-campus causes of the tuition crisis: declining teaching loads, . . . bloated administrative hierarchies, . . . and inflated course offerings." Banta (1999) summarizes these views when she states, "Never before has higher education been subjected to such close scrutiny by public stakeholders."

Higher education's response to much of this scrutiny has taken the form of initiatives to assess institutional effectiveness and student learning outcomes. Such quality assessment efforts that have focused specifically on community colleges include the League for Innovation in the Community College's Institutional Effectiveness Task Force and accompanying monograph (Doucette and Hughes, 1990), and "Learning Outcomes for the 21st Century Project" (Wilson, Miles, Baker, and Schoenberger, 2000); the American Association of Community Colleges' monograph *Core Indicators of Effectiveness for Community Colleges* (Alfred, Ewell, Hudgins, and McClenney, 1999); and the National Center for Higher Education Management Systems monograph *Assessment in Community Colleges: Setting the Standard for Higher Education?* (Banta, 1999).

Implied in these initiatives, in addition to internal measurement and analysis of intrainstitutional trends, is the expectation that at some point, colleges will be able to focus externally, to gauge themselves against similar data from comparable institutions. Sources for such benchmark data and information are nonexistent for the community college sector. On the other hand, benchmark data have been collected routinely for four-year colleges and universities by data-sharing consortia such as the Association of American Universities Data Exchange, the Higher Education Data Sharing Consortium, and the Southern Universities Group. However, these data are limited in scope and shared solely among members of the respective consortia; membership in those consortia is restricted and exclusive, and none includes community colleges. Thus, there are no data-collection or reporting processes among peer institutions for community colleges on a national basis.

In response to this set of circumstances, Johnson County (Kansas) Community College (JCCC) has taken a leadership role in two national community college benchmarking initiatives. The first of these is an effort to establish a consortium of an initial 100–200 two-year colleges nationwide to collect and report data involving instructional costs and productivity. Specifically, this three-year project, known as "the Kansas Study" and supported by a $282,113 grant from the U.S. Department of Education's Fund for the Improvement of Postsecondary Education (FIPSE), involves the development and implementation of a data-collection methodology and reporting process that will establish a comprehensive national interinstitutional community college faculty cost and productivity database. This database will allow community colleges to analyze faculty workload in a manner that enables them to describe what types of courses faculty teach, and at what cost, at the academic discipline level of analysis. Moreover, the database will allow institutions to compare their academic and fiscal resource utilization patterns with those of peer institutions. The overarching objective of the project is to provide a new management tool that will enable community colleges to make more informed resource allocation and reallocation decisions, enhancing overall productivity and cost-effectiveness. College faculty and administrators will be able to make internal decisions based on costs and productivity at the program level. In addition, this tool will aid institutions' efforts to assess institutional effectiveness and provide accountability through comparison of costs and productivity with peer-group benchmarks.

The Kansas Study is currently in the design phase. A project advisory committee has been formed, proposed data elements have been identified, and data definitions and a data-collection methodology have been developed. The study is being tested by approximately twelve community colleges. The pilot test will continue through summer 2003, and a rollout of the project to 50–100 participating institutions is planned for fall 2003. An additional 50–100 colleges will be added to the consortium in the academic year 2004–2005.

The second initiative, the National Community College Benchmarking Project, involves the development and implementation of an effort designed to institutionalize a national community college benchmark data-collection and information-sharing process. The project will create a national database accessible to any community college willing to share relevant information on a variety of instructional outcomes, continuing education, workforce development, and other core activities. While there is currently no process for gathering data on these core mission components in two-year colleges, a small-scale prototype is in the initial design stage. This prototype was initiated by JCCC and is being supported by a small amount of seed funding from JCCC, a group of eleven other two-year colleges, and the League for Innovation in the Community College. Representatives from these colleges and the league have formed a preliminary Community College Benchmark Task Force. The initial planning phase of the task force involves identifying data elements; determining data definitions; and designing data-collection protocol, methodology, and reporting strategies. The purpose of this project, guided by institutional experience with this small-scale prototype, is to develop a greatly expanded national model for collection, analysis, and dissemination of community college benchmark data. The project will be tested in summer 2003 and implemented at full scale in fall 2003. A proposal has been submitted to FIPSE for funds to support this project as well.

The underlying purpose for both of these projects is to address a crucial data and information gap for community college faculty, academic planners, and senior managers, for whom no reliable source currently exists. Availability of this type of data will facilitate both intrainstitutional and interinstitutional comparisons, aiding institutions' efforts to assess institutional effectiveness. Requests for additional information on either of these efforts, as well as inquiries about participation in either consortium, can be addressed to the author. Tel: (913) 469–8500, extension 3442. E-mail: <jseybert@jccc.net>.

References

Alfred, R., Ewell, P., Hudgins, J., and McClenney, K. *Core Indicators of Effectiveness for Community Colleges*. (2nd ed.) Washington, D.C.: Community College Press, 1999.

"America's Best Colleges." *U.S. News and World Report*, Sept. 19, 1996, pp. 91–105.

Banta, T. W. *Assessment in Community Colleges: Setting the Standard for Higher Education?* Boulder, Colo.: National Center for Higher Education Management Systems, 1999.

Doucette, D., and Hughes, B. *Assessing Institutional Effectiveness in Community Colleges*. Mission Viejo, Calif.: League for Innovation in the Community College, 1990.

Rosovsky, H. "From the Belly of the Whale." *Pew Policy Perspectives*, Sept. 1992, 4(3), A1–A8, B1–B4.

Wilson, C. D., Miles, C. L., Baker, R. L., and Schoenberger, R. L. *Learning Outcomes for the 21st Century: Report of a Community College Study*. Mission Viejo, Calif.: League for Innovation in the Community College, 2000.

Zemsky, R. and Massy, W. "Cost Containment: Committing to a New Economic Reality." *Change*, 1990, *22*(6), 16–22.

Jeffrey A. Seybert is director of research, evaluation, and instructional development at Johnson County Community College in Overland Park, Kansas, and serves as project director for both the Kansas Study and the National Community College Benchmarking Project.

The Wisconsin Technical College System Institutional Effectiveness Model

Donald Bressler, Deborah Mahaffey

The authors describe one of the nation's first systemwide models for measuring institutional effectiveness—a model that takes into account a broad range of core indicators that faculty could use to respond to accountability initiatives, accreditation demands, federal reporting requirements, and quality management initiatives. From Assessment Update *10:4.*

Context for the WTCS Model

Many colleges have developed a model for assessing institutional effectiveness (IE), but the Wisconsin Technical College System (WTCS) was among the first in the nation to develop a systemwide model. The challenge rested not just in identifying specific indicators but also in achieving consensus on a core of indicators that would guide systemwide *and* institutional improvement efforts. The WTCS presidents and the state governing agency agreed to create a model that concurrently provided a measure of effectiveness of the system as a whole while honoring the autonomous nature of each of the sixteen colleges in the statewide system. In order to accomplish the task of implementing an acceptable IE model with a meaningful outcome, two key elements were imperatives in the process: cross-functional collaboration and representative consensus.

The WTCS is governed by a board appointed by Wisconsin's governor. A director hired by the board heads a state agency that provides system leadership. Each technical college is directed by a president hired by a local board. The college presidents work together, along with the state agency, under a formal structure called the Administrators Association. The structure includes subcommittees for each of the administrative entities, including instructional services, student services, research and planning, and administrative/financial services. In addition, numerous systemwide meetings are conducted, manager-level committee meetings are held, and ad hoc groups are created to address timely issues, recommend uniform practices, and undertake collaborative efforts. Collaboration is a valued way of doing business.

The colleges have embraced a collaborative approach to program evaluation. The systemwide evaluation model set forth in the 1980s incorporated three phases: *accountability* through annual monitoring and screening data to indicate the general health of a program; *evaluation* through in-depth assessment of programs and services; and *impact appraisal* through assessment of "value-added" dimensions of the program or service. Further, the WTCS as a system has a long history of conducting employer satisfaction surveys and longitudinal studies of graduate employment status to assess program success.

Development of the Model

In 1992, the WTCS Administrators Association and the state agency agreed to contract cooperatively with outside consultants to help develop a tailor-made IE model. The project was undertaken as a systemwide effort to identify core indicators that could be used locally by colleges to respond to accountability initiatives, accreditation demands, federal reporting requirements, and quality management initiatives. The development process was intentionally designed to be inclusive and to achieve consensus across the technical college system.

One of the first steps centered on creating a task force with representation from various subgroups of the Administrators Association, the state agency, and other key stakeholders, including faculty unions. It was the mission of the Institutional Effectiveness Task Force to provide guidance and direction for the development of the model. Inclusiveness was paramount to the process. The task force assembled more than twenty face-to-face focus groups to obtain input from primary stakeholders regarding (1) key institutional characteristics of performance outcomes that define effectiveness in the technical college system and (2) indicators and data-gathering methods recommended for measuring effectiveness.

Focus groups included college presidents; students; college board members; union groups; faculty and support staff; college vice presidents; administrators for instruction, student services, adult education, economic development, research and planning, administrative services, and marketing; and state agency staff. The focus-group activities produced a list of more than one hundred potential effectiveness indicators. The next round of input, via written survey, sifted the indicators down to what were considered the primary IE indicators.

Ultimately, seventeen indicators focused on four categories of effectiveness: student achievement and satisfaction, employer satisfaction, organizational quality, and public perception and satisfaction. The exhibit at right shows the specific effectiveness indicators associated with each category.

Working with the Model

A new cross-functional steering team was established to provide the systemwide leadership and coordination necessary for moving from developing the model to adopting and implementing it. Clearly, the first stage had been inclusive of all customers, both internal and external to the technical colleges; this stage was time-consuming and thorough, if not laborious. Yet no one questioned the need for building all the right connections. Buy-in and consensus building take time and were recognized to be essential for the model to be credible and viable.

Leadership from the state agency and three college administrative areas—instruction, student services, and research and planning—made up the Institutional Effectiveness Steering Team. The team placed emphasis on continuing the focus on the Institutional Effectiveness Model

(IEM); establishing priorities based on identified college needs; ensuring integration of data-collection systems; facilitating collective improvements in accountability measures; and coordinating cooperative endeavors. The work began by focusing on student achievement and success—not an unreasonable choice given that each college faced an external accreditation mandate to develop a plan for assessing student achievement. It was easy to see the gains to be achieved through collaboration. The work was to be carried out through cross-functional work groups. Work-group membership and responsibilities were structured to ensure success: (1) individual members interfaced with college planning processes to integrate the results of IE measures with institutional improvement efforts; (2) membership included key stakeholders—representatives from all colleges, various college functions, and the state agency; (3) there was a consistent process for presenting the charge and mission to each work group; (4) each work group used an effective process-improvement strategy; (5) there was interaction with other appropriate groups and initiatives with related functional responsibilities; and (6) each work group had a limited focus and scope of measurement.

Three work groups were created to focus on seven of the indicators relating to student assessment and achievement. Each of the three work groups (student goals at entry and exit; student functional skills at entry and exit; and course completion, retention, and graduation) were chaired by a steering team member and charged with the task of making recommendations for effective implementation of the indicators at the college level, the state level, or both.

During the next two years, more than fifty-five individuals from across the state worked collaboratively on cross-functional work groups. These groups refined definitions of effectiveness indicators, clarified parameters, and offered recommendations to operationalize indicators at the college and statewide levels. The outcomes have been impressive. For example, the cross-functional work group on student goals piloted an instrument and process for assessing student goals at entry and suggesting points of interaction based on student needs. The approach of the cross-functional work group dealing with assessment of students' functional skills at entrance and exit produced a philosophical grounding for assessment activities, a "menu of options" for assessment, and a database on current practices with the WTCS. The work group on student retention and withdrawal rates and course completion and graduation rates developed standard definitions for terms and core analysis methods for the purpose of monitoring and assessment. It is important to understand that before recommendations were advanced and considered as final work-group products, individual members of each work group shared preliminary recommendations with their respective colleagues to gain consensus on direction and to generate buy-in for full adoption and use of the recommendations. Those actions were considered to be standard process steps and at the heart of the rollout process.

Progress to Date

The accomplishments of the three initial work groups served as a good starting point and springboard for the IEM. In fall 1997, a WTCS assessment conference was held to serve as a celebration of accomplishments, a forum for sharing assessment practices among individual colleges, and an opportunity to report on the status of the development of the IEM. All sixteen colleges participated, and the conference evaluations called for "doing this again."

The Administrator's Association has called for development of a comprehensive plan for systemwide implementation of all IE indicators. The IE Steering Team has promulgated a final deployment plan endorsed by the Administrators Association that calls for alignment with current evaluation models and practices. Further, the plan continues to rely heavily on systemwide collaboration. Intact administrative committees and targeted cross-functional groups have been asked to review current practices and collaboratively recommend "best practice(s)" related to the other areas of the IEM: employer satisfaction, organizational quality, and public perception and satisfaction.

Clearly, the work is not done. But, most important, the work done to date has been based on collaboration and consensus. The commitment is there. The benefits have been significant and meaningful in terms of both product and process. The work will continue to be refined and ad-

Assessment UPdate
COLLECTIONS

Assessment Update Collections provide readers with information on specific areas of assessment—gathered together for the first time in a single, easy-to-use booklet format. Specially selected by editor Trudy W. Banta from the rich archives of *Assessment Update*, the articles in these booklets represent the best thinking on various topics and are chosen to ensure that readers have information that is relevant and comprehensive and illustrates effective practice. **Ordering information:** Each booklet costs $14.95 and can be ordered by calling 888.378.2537 or visiting our Web site at www.josseybass.com. Want to order additional copies of this booklet? Call Lora Templeton at 415.782.3127 for information on our bulk discounts.

Portfolio Assessment This booklet's articles explore how portfolios, including Web-based portfolios, have been used at various institutions to assess and improve programs in general education, the major, advising, and overall institutional effectiveness. They describe ways portfolios can be scored, students' perspectives on portfolios, how portfolios changed the faculty culture at one college, and more. 80 pages ISBN 0-7879-7286-X

Community College Assessment Nowhere is the need for assessment methods of demonstrated value felt more strongly than at the community college. This booklet gathers together for the first time some of the best illustrations of good practice available, addressing such issues as evaluating transfer success, assessing employer needs, community and technical college students' perceptions of student engagement, corporate partnerships in assessment, and much more. 74 pages ISBN 0-7879-7287-8

Hallmarks of Effective Outcomes Assessment This booklet brings together the best guidance and practices from *Assessment Update* to illustrate time-tested principles for all aspects of assessment from planning and implementing to sustaining and improving assessment efforts over time. Useful for those new to assessment as well as experienced practitioners, it details the specific hallmarks required for the success of any assessment program—from leadership and staff development to the assessment of processes as well as outcomes, ongoing communication among constituents, and more. 72 pages ISBN 0-7879-7288-6

About the Editor: Trudy W. Banta is vice chancellor for planning and institutional improvement at Indiana University-Purdue University Indianapolis and editor of the bimonthly *Assessment Update: Progress, Trends, and Practices in Higher Education*. She has written or edited 10 published volumes on assessment, including *Assessment Essentials*, with Catherine Palomba (Jossey-Bass, 1999) and *Building a Scholarship of Assessment* (Jossey-Bass, 2002). Banta has been honored for her work by the National Council on Measurement in Education, the American Association for Higher Education, the American Productivity and Quality Center, and the Association for Institutional Research.